Trench Town Rock

Selected Titles by Kamau Brathwaite

Four Plays for Primary Schools (Longmans 1964)
Odale's choice (Evans 1967)
The Arrivants: A New World Trilogy (Oxford University
    Press 1973)
Days & Nights (Caldwell 1971)
Other Exiles (Oxford University Press 1975)
Black + Blues (Casa de las Americas 1976)
Mother Poem (Oxford University Press 1977)
Soweto (Savacou 1979)
Word Making Man: A Poem for Nicolás Guillén
    (Savacou 1979)
Sun Poem (Oxford University Press 1982)
Korabra (with paintings by Gavin Jantjes London, 1986)
Jah Music (Savacou 1986)
The Visibility Trigger (Cahiers de Louvain 1986)
X/Self (Oxford University Press 1987)
Sappho Sakyi's Meditations (Savacou 1989)
Shar (Savacou 1992)
Middle Passages (New Directions 1993)
Zea Mexican Diary (U. of Wisconsin Press 1993)
Roots: Literary Criticism (U. of Michigan 1993)

Kamau Brathwaite

Trench Town Rock

Lost Roads Publishers   Number 40   Providence 1994
Denver 2007

Library of Congress Cataloging in Publication Data
Brathwaite, Kamau, 1930–   Trench Town Rock
    (Lost Roads series; no. 40)
    I. Title

PS
ISBN 0-918786-54-1
    2007   cip 92-0954569
The author and the editors gratefully acknowledge Nathaniel
Mackey, the editor of *Hambone*, issue #10 of which published a
variant of this text.

First printing by McNaughton and Gunn
Cover photograph by Deborah Luster
Cover design by Duncan Barlow
Book design by Issa Clubb
Typeset by Issa Clubb, based on the 'Sycorax video-print' style of
Kamau Brathwaite

Special thanks to Michael Ondaatje in cooperation with the
Lannan Foundation for helping to make this publication possible.

This project is supported by a grant from the National Endowment
for the Arts in Washington, D.C., a federal agency.

This is Trench Town Rock
Don't watch that
Trench Town Rock
Big fish or sprat
Trench Town Rock
You reap what you sow
Trench Town Rock
And only Jah Jah know
Trench Town Rock
I never turn my back

Bob Marley *(1988)*

1. The Marley Manor Shoot/in

16 July 1990

Lass night about 2:45 well well well before the little black bell of the walk of my electronic clock cd wake me—

aweakened by gunshatt

—the eyes trying to function open too stunned to work out there through the window & into the dark with its various glints & glows: mosquito, very distant cockcrow, sound system drum, the tumbrel of a passing engine somewhere some/where in that dark. It must have been an ear/ring's earlier sound that sprawled me to the window. but it was

TWO SHATTS

—silence—

not evening the dogs barking or the trees blazing
& then a cry we couldn't see of

do

do

do

nuh kill me

answeared by a volley of some

SEVEN

crack-like-firecracker-racket shats & then a soundless figure fleeing like on air towards the right of sound perhaps towards the fence or laundry?

Silence

The eyes like thir/sty out there in the dark & then two males—two malés—high steppin through the street-lit gateway of the Marley Manor & quickly joined by a (?wounded) lagging third. I watch them walk down Marley's Road... then they begin to run...

10 minutes late—not later—longer—white headlights—

<<THE POLICE>>

the whole place crawling plainclothes cops

whose finger on which blind frightened trigger of a telephone had beckoned them?

eventually three soldiers in full battledress of olive leaves. the ariels of their walkie-talkies bending the night sky skye like breeze like bamboos...and like ants, it sadly seemed...their cars to car/casses...

Xcept that ants are never late as these now were too late although they came, their welcome rumbling in—so many now—*I had not thought death had undone so many*—& even then their radios were blaring out... *three men on Hope Road armed & dangerous... a door kick-off at Stannpipe... another traffic axe...* & all the other rapes & burns & murthers taking place all over Kingston in the kingdom of this world...

From down my upstairs window I cd see all this. like opposite the Marley gateway to so sudden swiftly

HELL

where just a world before there had been laughter splashing in the pool, reverb & ghetto-box, Red Stripe, bells softly sing/ing sing/ing, somebody sucking cane & shouting out dem dancehall business in the dark—if only Mr Crook wd oversee the cutting of him *bush* we wd have seen the whole court/yard, the bleak car/park & more—the stark lawns to the right obscured by almond leaves where I had seen the 'person' running running running down that first loud waking valley of the

SHARKS

Now/at the wild white Marley gateway, there is a little matching dolly house where our 'security guard'—well—*sleeps*. Seeing no light come on in there despite the shats, I wondered & was worried Might it have been him I saw there *running* out there just that while ago?... & only yesterday he'd been the boss in here...

him own gun cracking off sometimes at night & next day we wd hear the story of how he'd almost *shat a one*... but now that cry & silence & my worry for him beating in the silence, my heart like in my eyes & bandage & beating till it hurt as if my pain was his inside my head & bondage...

The police had driven straight in, jumping out their cars & jeeps with salaams & slams & semi-automatic acks, revolvers slung from belts & holsters or tucked like asps into their waist-line trousers; & evvabody walkin fass fass fass, some runnin, plenty movemant, their flashlights in their hands like little ashen candles—

All Souls

As we approach the guard's dull house anxious to find out why it was not now lit up—like it was either him out there or somewhere dead—*do do nuh kill me*—or had he run away(?)—perhaps he hadn't even come to work at all *on this momentous night O God help us* and what was it that Chad first saw—like lying part-way on the curb between its whitelime border & the grass that curved away towards that palisade where we had seen ?his shadow fleeing—do you remember?—into this bundle of like nothing now—this dirty clot—this empty silent clothing...

Was a young dreadlocks [later I was to learn that he was known as "Early Bird"/catching his first too early worm of death that early All Souls Mourning] **his beautiful long hair like curled around his body making snakes like dance/like**

dancing. the seven bullet holes that walked us from our sleep all bleeding in the early morning light. One rebok trainer some way off. as if it had been cut off from his body in the terror. & his hair—some of his hair—his locks—beside him—pulled out by the very roots by some strange/some strange strangar violence—the gunmen had been dragging him away like that by all his loveliness. his body now without its bones or muscleature. without its meat without its clutch & nomen of a face/familiar creatures/that someone somewhere somehow knew/that someone/somewhere loved & because the man himself had fled out through these leaking holes, his locks had whirled around him as the bullets made him dance his death & wrapped themselves around him as he fell. so now there was this eerie beauty in the barley light. his hair become his only perhaps comforter

Mystery killings at Apartment complex

As the latest wave of killings in the Corporate Area continues, three men, including a policeman, were slain at an apartment complex in the Kingston 6 area in the early hours of Sunday morning. Two of them were tied with their hands behind their backs, then shot in the head.

Residents in the area heard shots at about 2:30 a.m, and called the police. When the Police arrived at Marley Manor Apartments off Hope Road, they discovered the body of [but that was later...]

Further investigation revealed the body of the apartment security guard inside his station, with his hands tied.
The Daily Gleaner Monday, July 16, 1990, p1

es he was dead in there (though second not third found), the door locked in upon him, lights not on—

now on—

he crumpled down upon his back upon the narrow
cement floor
his hands tied up behind his back
his feet like under him & also bound
the dead eyes staring
the face not even twisted by the fatal blow
a big red plop and poppy on his chest
among the hairs
still thick & softly leaking out & leaking out & leaking out

his chair half-broken with the sudden soundless
blackward crash

And then with the sun coming up, right on the green
embankment underneath my window, between, in
fact, the frieze my car made with the bank, so
squeezed & un-

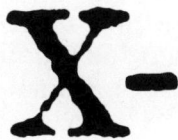

pected there that no police had seen it with their can-
dles, was a third: blue jeans, chest naked, hands
bound behind his back with

TWO DISHCLOTHS

— for goodness sake—
taken no doubt from the Marley Manor clothesline—

with the sun coming up coming up coming up the
police ask—no—order me—abrupt & violent as any
crime—to roll my cyar away & then they rolled him
over like a stone & from the stain of dark green blood

upon our grass & sepulchre & untied his dishcloth
hands behind his back and let his arms fall
free—

a police—big, dark, meaty guy whose job, it seems,
was checking on security at MMA
But I can't tell you what he looked like: features,
the human face, I mean: both eyes shot out/stabbed
in, his nose unhinged, a huge gash in the right side
of the throat, his tongue there black & smooth &
half-leaf out his face as if he'd
strangled also
yet all his skin & flesh still firm & natural
like if he flash & living still & not a ant or insect
coming even near his blood & no one say a
prayer—at least out loud—nor paused—

O Sodom & Gomorrah—

nor raised a hum or hymn for anyone—for anyone
of us—that night/that early morning sun/day

And by the two o'clock midday TV news my poor blue cyar the same 'poor cyar' that wd some nine weeks later (see below) be stolen from me from this same sad place. at this same level time of gunpoint dawn & I wd think aloud that it was grey—the colour of the light inside me on that morn **was on 'the air' as if it/self had carried out the crime & all day long there was this trek of visits to 'the scene'**

click/click
gape/gossip
even though the
bodies & their
silence of potato
sacks had long
been thrown into
the dark blue
police vans. the
dark blood hosed
away…

This the 309th dead by gunshot in 6½ months in Kingston in the kingdoom of this world; on 15 Aug 90 the Police High Command, having said a few weeks earlier that 'Crime was under control', announced that since the begrinning of the year, there had been some 3000 crimes recorded in Jamaica—how many many not!— inc 357 murders

Last night's tv glimpsed us a picture of the Spanish Town morgue where children's bodies were piled up like at Belsen or Auschwitz. The object of this particular xercise was to show us the bodies of two children murdered in their home while their mother was at Church last Sunday ?night (12 Aug 90). Brother & sister, aged 8 and 10 & naked in the picture to the bone, had been stabbed 25 times/each—But no—the newspaper report (17 Aug 90) is much more boggling. The boy, Darian, was actually 18 (not 8) years old & he was stabbed—by ice-pick—not 25 but 70. His sister, Allecia, 140 times...

17 Aug is Marcus Garvey Birthday

the same day (1983) that poet Mikey Smith was stoned
to death on Stony Hill

By the end of October 1990

622 Violent Deaths

'More than 620 people died violently up to the end of October, making this the most violent year since 1980 [when 889 people died violently in that Election year].

'Figures compiled from police reports show that a total of 622 people were shot, stabbed with a knife or icepick, hacked to death with a machette, or bludgeoned with a blunt instrument. Murders totalled 469 – 242 persons were killed by guns and 109 by knives.

'In addition to the murders, 153 fatal shootings have been recorded in the year's first 10 months: 133 by police, 20 by civilians...

'If the average of almost 47 murders per month continues, the country could record a total over 550 murders by the end of December. [The two months June & July – the 'Independence holiday season' – totalled a high of 167 murders, because a/c to Dep Police Commissioner Bertram Millwood i/c of Crime, of the "existing high spirits and criminals' need for more spending money during the approaching Independence holiday season"]

'Millwood added that the lifting of the Suppression of Crime Act in May in Kingston, St Andrew and St Catherine, coupled with a period of feuding between rival gangs and fighting for leadership among gang members, may also have contributed to the two-month spurt.'
The Sunday Gleaner, Gordon C Williams 11 Nov 1990, p1

in addition
there are an equal number of/if not more violent
deaths on the road—inc 229 children killed

at noon 10 Dec 90 JBC TV announced fatality no
375

—not to mention all the physical & psychological
damage & maiming—
+
one rape every 8 hours: 1000+ reported cases of
abuse & rape last year 44 reported cases of incest
all in a population just barely 2.3+ million
+

'Early Bird' buried

Hundreds of Matthews Lane community members, including relatives, close friends and curious onlookers, turned out to say their last farewell to
Glenford St Joseph Phipps
"Early Bird"
on Wednesday at the
All Saints Church, West Street, Kingston.

Bird, a former supervisor at Metropolitan Parks and Markets(MPM) and "a godfather" to many in the Matthews Lane community in downtown Kingston,
was paid
glowing tributes at the service, which saw a wide cross-section of well-known people in attendance.

A close relative of Bird who resides overseas, called on members of the congregation to dismiss the idea of "revenge". He quoted a line from the scripture: "A soft answer turneth away wrath, but grievous words stirreth anger."

"We miss you, we love you," he cried. "My friends, death ends life, but not a relationship."

Bird's brother, Kevin, described him as a man who lived a "moral life" of principles, a courageous soldier, and one who always cried peace.

He said that Bird was a person who always sought to "defuse tension, rather than add to it."

Greta Robinson, general manager of MPM who worked closely with Bird, described him as "a special person to all of us, a brother and a son who was always there when everybody was in need of help."

Bird was inspirational in setting up the Matthews United Basic School, later changed to Bird's name (in memory of him). The church was filled to capacity and family members and friends were overcome with grief at different stages of the service...

Bird is survived by mother, Sunshine, nine children, six brothers, three sisters and a host of other relatives.

Phipps was shot and killed on Sunday July 15, when gunmen

invaded his Marley Manor apartment.
He was found dead in the
driveway, with bullet wounds to
the head. A security guard and a
policeman were also killed in the attack.
The Jamaica Record, Fri 27 July, 1990

This clipping
was sent to a friend of mine in
London
It was sent by a friend (?) of mine in Jamaica
a poet & a writer!
who knew/who knows that I was/am
(?) living here
& therefore possibly in danger of dying here
that fatal foreday morning

**Yet in that covering letter
w/ the clip. the clipping
there is no. not a single reference
to me. my presence
myself in danger possibly
no flick or feather of concern**

So that these crimes we *all* embrace
the victim & the violate
the duppy & the gunman
so close on these plantations still
so intimate
the dead/undead

2. Straight Talk

19 July 1990

ttortt

When last did you see your Father?

Police reports state that 120 persons were detained and I have a list ere in front of me, Mr Perkins, where one undred an *two* of the undread & twenty persons that were detained

Perkins: Yes

—   came from the Rema area alone

Perkins: Yes

—   **Now I doan know what sort a operation dat is**

[This is the JLP Councillor & Caretaker for the Rema area of West Kingston speaking to Wilmot (Motty/Mutty) Perkins, the host of the KLAS FM/Manchester (Jamaica) radio talk show, *Straight Talk*, on the midday of 19 July 90

—   **But despite all a dat, Mr Perkins, despite de/despite de/de/de/de detention of de people Mr Perkins, I want to make it clear, Mr Perkins, that we are not against raids & search & curfew to stem the gun voiolence, we are not against it; what we are against, Mr Perkins, is the attitude of the Military towards individual there yesterday and I'm going to tell you some of the things that took place there yesterday**

[Meanwhile on TV, young Tivoli women speak in loud quarreling voices of the *rat-foot soldiers*— the *rat patrol soldiers* —dat *come up in ere* shooting & abusin people; one dahta tells the camera how she was juss comin back from the supermar-

29

ket with she ten-month baby when the shooting star & she was *so fraid* she like she *tun fool* & run pass she mudda ouse & buck up inna smaddy else yord & the baby it im ead before she study <steady> sheself & fine out wha gwaan]

When the men were taken from their ouses, Mr Perkins... they were axed to drape each other in their pants waist

Perkins: Yes—

—   **You box me, I box you; I kiss you, you kiss me**

Perkins: Kiss?

—   **Kiss, Mr Perkins. Kiss like ow a man kiss/a woman. The soldiers/instruct/ the men/tokiss/each other**

Perkins: You saw this happening?

—   **This is a fac, Mr Perkins**

Perkins: I'm asking—

—   **Mr Perkins—**

Perkins: I'm asking you—

—   **Mr—**

Perkins: Hold on!

—   **Mr Perkins—**

Perkins: Who says—

—   **I did not see it with my own two eyes, Mr. Perkins, but the—**

Perkins:	Hold—
—	persons oou were *victims* of it, Mr Perkins, I spoke with one such person lass night and that person is prepared to come out an say it. I have a *number* of statements here in front of me—
Perkins:	Uhuh
—	Not only the kissing alone, Mr Perkins. They were axed, Mr Perkins, the men were axed to rub up themselves on each other
Perkins:	No Mr—
—	No no Mr Perkins, this is not a *joke*, Mr Perkins
Perkins:	**Mr McKenzie!**
McKenzie:	Yes sir
Perkins:	Hold on likkle bit now. [Pause]. **Now:** I remember hearing stories like these, coming, as it happened, from the other side, because in those days in 1980
McKenzie:	Yes
Perkins:	it was held that the police & soldiers had turned against the then Government, right?
McKenzie:	Yes
Perkins:	as we were coming to the elections and I heard allegations like these

McKenzie: Yes

Perkins: made on JBC radio & television—

McKenzie: Yes

Perkins: against the—which was then—as Mr Seaga described it—a PNP cesspool

McKenzie: Yes

Perkins: I heard stories like these—

McKenzie: Yes—

Perkins: being told against the soldiers in that year, right? Nothing ever came of it, nobody ever did anything about it, nobody ever preferred any allegations in any formal way about it

McKenzie: Yes—

Perkins: I now hear it coming from the *other political* side—

McKenzie: Well this is not a political sityation now, Mr. Perkins

Perkins: Now hold on—

McK: Mr Perkins, this—what I am saying to you now—

Perkins: I have to be very skeptical about stories like this–

McK: Mr Perkins! Mr Perkins! There's *nutten* to be skeptical about... Mr Perkins, there is one report here I ave

	in front of me, where the men were axed to lie down in the grass, eat the dry grass, some were forced to eat plastic bag, and some were forced to eat—ah—faeces—dog faeces. This is not a jokin matter, Mr Perkins
P:	No—Mr McKenzie—
	[Perkins had in fact retailed a similar story just before McKenzie phoned]
McK:	Mr Perkins, Mr Perkins, I doan call you all de way from Kingston [KLAS, remember, originates in Mandeville] to score cheap political points; that is not what I call you about
P:	No Mr McKenzie. Mr/Mr/Mr [pause] McKenzie
McK:	Yes sah
P:	I think—you know—I wonder—whether what should happen, is that the political representatives from these areas should not make an attempt to be present—who/who is the MP for/for/for this—for that—area at the moment?
McK:	Minister Jones, Bobby Jones...
	[an earlier caller when asked this Q had said that there was no MP for the area & Perkins had told her that that was because she was JLP and was not recognizing the PNP MP]
P:	Bobby Jones...I wonder whether Mr. Bobby Jones should not have been

making/or whether the MPs in the particular area, should not be making an attempt to be present when these operations are going on—just to observe, just to observe—and to be able to go–

[Perkins' point is that the MPs and the political reps and the Press shd be present during these searches—not interfering—but being eye-witnesses and referees to what was going on, so that cases of brutality, if such they were, wd be observed, monitored & officially/publicly reported etc. That the Press shd find ways to 'get in there' & do their work, despite the reported abuse & smashing of cameras by soldiers; and that the soldiers were in any case acting illegally in searching and detaining people in view of the repeal of the Suppression of Crimes Act just a few weeks ago—a repeal, some people say, which is responsible for the flare up of violence in the 'Inner City' areas such as Tivoli, Rema, Fletcher's Land [and now/1 August 90] West Road & Matches Lane etc/to such a degree that the Suppression of Crimes Act has been RE/INTRODUCED for a period of 30 days] and attorney at law and Human Rights activist, Dennis Daley had come on *Straight Talk* and declared that all present and indeed past police action in detaining people (from 'the deprived areas') was illegal and that he wished that somebody wd bring a court action against the Security Forces for this and not long after, on the 6pm News, we heard that Mr Seaga was doing just that—a Court action against the Attorney General and the Commissioner of Police and Brig Gen Neish]. McKENZIE COUNTERED WITH...

McK: **Well... I wear two caps as I speak to you. I'm the Councillor for Tivoli and the JLP Caretaker for that constituency. When Tivoli Gardens was cordon on Monday, I came down, I went to the soldier, I was very polite, I identified myself an/an e told me in a very**

	polite but a forceful manner dat you/you cannot enter into the area! So regardless of your status, Mr Perkins—
P:	Yes
McK:	the treatment dat dey are anding out to people dere—
P:	Yes
McK:	Ah/I was dere when they assaulted de/de *Record* reporter—
P:	Yes
McK:	I saw it on Darling Street, an dat was not fictitious, it was a fac—
P:	You saw it happen?
McK:	Yes! I saw it!

[The day before Motty had dedicated nearly his whole programme to fulminating against this incident; he even had Brig General Neish and the Commissioner of Police on the line to answer questions… though neither of them, 'up the news time', as it were, had been officially informed of the incident but admitted that if it had happened as reported, that it was reprehensible and punishable—Motty wanted to know if the soldiers wd be court-martialled & they said they wd certainly look into it and act if necessary as quickly as possible]

McK:	It was a fact! [Pause]. And the point I'm making to you now, Mr Perkins is that the incidents that took place in Rema—I thought the people in Tivoli Gardens during that curfew on Monday was treated badly, but what was

dun to de people in REMA yesterday M/M/Mr Perkin, is beyonn a all—no human be'en, Mr. Perkins deserve to be treated in dat way and a want to take you back, Mr. Perkins, to 1976, Mr. Perkin when those very same people, Mr. Perkins, were victims of invasions where they furnitures, their/their personal property was destroyed and they were thrown out of doors in 1976, Mr Perkins.

Mr Perkins, what took place there yesterday is a total/disgrace and/and Mr Perkins, there is no way you can pinpoint a soldier to say dat dis is de soldier dat did it because the soldiers doan carry numbers! The soldiers doan carry anyting dat you can i/dentify dem to say dat dis is de man oou/oou did it! M/M Mr Perkins, what I am saying to you is not fictitious, it is not done to score political points, it is someting dat took place, I am speaking about REALITY, someting dat took place yesterday

[Perkins now (his voice calm & assured) repeats (develops) his point about Police/Soldier illegality, the need to have the Press present regardless, and above all for MPs to be present—not to interfere—but so that they cd OBSERVE & report what was happening back to Parliament /which is 'the body responsible' and he didn't think that any soldier had the RIGHT to go and interfere with any Parliamentarian...]

Perkins: I don't think that the soldiers & police cd have any right to exclude a parliamentarian from there, I am not say—

[At this point, McKenzie interrupts with]

McK: **Well Mr Perkins I don't think that that sorta privilege has been afforded to anybody—**

P: [getting xcited] **No! is not a matter—No No No No!—Hole on likkle bit!—No! Mr/ Mr/Mr McKenzie doan tell me *rubbish*—**

McK: But Mr Perkins—

P: **Hole on a minit—**

McK: Mr—

P: **BUT HOLE ON!**

McK: But Mr Perkins—

P: **YOU HOLE ON A—**

McK: Mr Perkins—

Perkins: [louder & louder]

Mr McKenzie, you lissen to me!

McK: Mr Perkins, dat sort a—

Perkins: **Mr McKenzie, you lissen to me!**

McK: If/if in my office—

P: [sucking his teeth and pretty close to apoplexy now]

O lissen to me or/or we stop this conversation!

McK: Go ahead, go ahead

P: Parliament makes the laws in this country...

Conversation ends with this bittle classic

McK: There is a youngster in custody from Monday—an I wan' you to unnerstann ow far dis ting go, you know Mr. Perkins. We ave a patient—e is asthmatic. Is name is Andrew Williams. E was taken out of is sick bed on Monday by the military & the police & e was taken away. Is mother was able to fine im lass night at the AlfWay Tree Police Station

P: Yes

McK: When she went in, she brought some tablets for im. The police say e cyaaan get the tablets, doctor ave to approve the tablet before im can get it An when they finally decide to release the fellow, when e was coming out, a Superintendent Howell said to im—

'Where Jim Brown ide im gun?'

Lester Lloyd Coke, alias Jim Brown (also 'Jim', 'Big Man' [he was], 'Dads', 'Bomber', 'Don') of the gold-coloured Mercedes Benz (*Sun Gleaner*, 15 March 92, p3A) 'identified as a co-leader of [the] notorious [Miami-based] Shower Posse crime gang, has been in custody [in the General Penitentiary] awaiting extradition to the US to face murder charges' (*Ja Record* Sun Feb 9, 1992, p2A) [his partner, 'Storyteller' Morrison, held for the same charges at the same time, was 'accidentally'/'prematurely' sent back to the States & protests, pleas, diplomatic & court actions failed to budge the Americans] is apparently the present ruling *The-harder-they-come* Rhygin of the Corporate area, reputed gunman & political activist & 'Don Gorgon' wanted in the US on various charges & ?finally captured (1991) in Kingston in a paramilitary SEARCH+DESTROY ('Rat Patrol') OPERATION & is in police custody (some say 'custardy') here awaiting xtradition... But the word on the street is that **if dem deport Jim Brown to Amerika, Kingston go bun dung flat flat flat like a flat cake inna Bandung** & that a lot of the recent voiolence [July-Aug 90], inc that in the Coronation Market (& prob at MM) is connect w/ this

On 2 March 1992, JIM BROWN, about a week after his son Jah T was guNNED down on IM MOTOBIKE ON MAXWELL AVE in broad daylight (1 Feb 92)/d 2 Feb 92 & **400 WAS FE DEAD FE DAT** & the carnAGE had started—some 14 dead or injured—Brown was found 'incinerated' (some reports say DEAD FROM 'SMOKE INHALATION') in IM 'CUSTARDY'

A NUMBER of vendors in the CORONATION MARKET have complained to the *Gleaner* of being robbed of thousands of dollars at gunpoint on Saturday when, they said, over 30 gunmen from Tivoli Gardens invaded the place Higglers along Barry Street and other market streets in West Kingston have also claimed they, too, were robbed by the gunmen. **"At one time dem hol' up 20 woman and when dem no tek off dem apron fass enough dem cut dem off."**
[*Daily Gleaner*, 21 July 1990, p17]

Information reaching *The Jamaica Record* is that men were "moving around" yesterday warning vendors that they should clear the streets. A source told our newsroom that

"there is expected to be war tonight", "there will be a lot of gunshots"

our source said.

By August 1/Emancipation Day 1990, parts of west/downtown Kingston were in fact "locked down": daylight gunfire, banks, stores closed, no vendors on the street... While in Trinidad, Imam Yassim Abu Bakr's 100+ Black Muslims (Jamaat al-Muslimeen) were holding the Prime MInister of Trinidad & Tobago and some 42 other Parliamentarians & others hostage—Fri July 27—Wed 1 August—that same Emancipation Day that Iraq's Muslim President Saddam Hussein did what Abu Bakr failed to do when he stormed & overthrew the Royal Government of Kuwait 'in response to a popular uprising'—the consequences of this being yet another story...

'A visit to Spanish Town Road and its environs by our newsteam yesterday confirmed that some of the vendors were clearing the streets. This was at 4:30 pm yesterday afternoon. One vendor when asked why there was a hurry to leave the streets, said

"Gunmen a go shoot up the place."

Vendors were reluctant to speak to our newsteam. As one vendor put it,

"The gunman dem might a lissen to what we a say."

Unconfirmed reports are that gunmen **have about four youts** in their custody and that **[they] are expected to face a fate similar to the three youths... found dead on West Street yesterday...**

The bloodied bodies of Ricardo Saunders, 15, of 21 Foster Lane, Oniel Sewell, 18, of 11 Gold Street, and an unidentified youth known only as "Blacka" were found [yesterday morning] on a handcart on [Matches Lane], West Street near to the Redemption Market: all had gunshot wounds to the heads...'
[*Ja Record* 31 July 1990, p3]

—Don Gorgon's people trying to bring the country to ransom, as it were, in xchange for his body of freedom...and all this coevil, as it were, with the JAG SMITH CASE—the former (JLP) Minister of Labour & at the moment (July 90) still Opposition Senator (his seat was not given up until mid 1991) on public trial for—and the day after this conversation found guilty of—appropriating hundreds of thousands of dollars ($J490,000) from the 'poor-people' US & Canadian Farm-Workers Programme into him own pocket in the form of cash, cars, property & gifts for friends & family and sentenced to 5 years hard labour

'This man is a former Minister of Government [from a famous father & family], a person who was viewed as an ambassador for the country and for many years a man of integrity, a person who we as Jamaicans looked to for leadership and guidance'. Now guilty not of need but xcessive greed & 'displaying a reprehensible contempt for his colleagues, his Party, his forebears and his country...'

McK: **an de man seh, 'Sir, whatcha axin meh, I doan know dem sort a ting, so wha kind a foolishness yu axin meh'** an you know wha happen Mr Perkins?

P: Alright, okay

McK: **The Superintendent of Police—**

P: OK, hold on—

McK: **The Superintendent of Police—**

P: Mr McKenzie, I don't want you to make any allegations against the Superintendent of—

McK: **No, is not allegations! is not an allegation, Mr Perkins**

P: Okay

McK: **When e said e didn't know** [this is the same asthmatic Andrew Williams] **e was ordered back in the cell an e was told**

One more night in custody might refresh your memory ['Where Jim Brown ide im gun?'] So tomorrow morning yu mother can come back fe yow...

*transcribed the above interview from tape of radio programme cited. Wrote Mr Perkins for permish to reproduce it here; after sev months silence, phoned Motty at KLAS/FM/ Mandeville who generously gave GO AHEAD

DG of 16 May 1992 carries photo of Mr McKenzie, surrounded by concerned JLP leaders, lying on Hospital bed or slab of white after receiving what the Report said was 'a severe beating from unnamed 'political opponents'. The Police & JLP were 'investigating.'

3. Kingston in the kingdom of this world

Sept 1990

the wind blows on the hillside
       and i suffer the little children
i remember the lilies of the field
       the fish swim in their shoals of silence
our flung nets are high wet clouds drifting

with this reed i make music
with this pen i remember the word
with these lips i can remember the beginning of the world

between these bars is this sudden lock-up
       where there is only the darkness of dog-bark
       where i cannot make windmills of my hands
       where i cannot run down the hill-path of faith
       where i cannot suffer the little children

a man may have marched with armies
       he may have crossed the jordan and the red sea
       he may have stoned down the wells of jericho

here where the frogs creak where there is only the croak of starlight

he is reduced
he is reduced
he is reduced

                to a bundle of rags/a broken
                    stick
                that will never whistle through
                    fingerstops into the music
                        of flutes
                that will never fling nets/white
                      sails crossing

gospel was a great wind freedom of savannas
gospel was a great mouth telling thunder of heroes
gospel was a cool touch warm with the sunlight like

        water in claypots, healing
                this reduction wilts the flower
        weakens the water
                coarsens the lips

        fists at the bars, shake rattle &
        hammer at the locks

                suffer the little children
                suffer the rose gardens
                suffer the dark clouds
                howling for bread
                suffer the dead fish pois-
                      oned in the lake

my authority was sunlight: the man who arose from
        the dead called me saviour
        his eyes had known moons
        older than jupiters
my authority was windmills. choirs singing of the
flowers of rivers

your authority is these chains that strangle my wrists
your authority is the red whip that circles my head
your authority is the white eye of interrogator's
        terror. siren price fix the law of undarkness
        the dreadness of the avalanches of unjudgement

it is you who roll down boulders when I say word
it is you who cry wolf when i offer the peace
        of wood doves
it is you who offer up the silence of dead leaves

        i would call out but the guards do not listen
        i would call out but the dew out there on the
                grass cannot glisten
        i would call out but my lost children
                cannot unshackle their shadows of silver

                    here i am reduced
                              to this hole of my head
                    where i cannot cut wood
                              where i cannot eat bread
                    where i cannot break fish
                              with the multitudes

my authority was foot-stamp upon the ground
          the curves the palms the dancers
my authority was nyambura inching closer
          embroideries of fingers. silver earrings balancers

                              but i am reduced
                                        i am reduced
                                        i am reduced

                              to these black eyes
                              this beaten face
                              these bleach-
                              ing lips blear-
                              ing obscenities

          i am reduced
          i am reduced
          i am reduced
                              to this damp
                              to this dark
                              to this driven
                              rag

                                        awaiting
                              the water of sun/light
                                        awaiting
               the lilies to spring up out of the iron
                                        awaiting
                    your eyes o my little children

                                             awaiting

4.
My turn

Foreday morning
Wednesday, October 24 1990

Get back here safe [from Bdos] only to run into a two-gunman break-in (actually one gun/one knife—one of my sharpest kitchen knives is missing…/**& were they more outside? lookhouts, get-away or back-up drivers, duppies, warriors, drones?**]) at my Marley Manor apartment in the early hours of Wednesday morning (Oct 24)—the same apartment complex where only 90 days ago there was a posse shoot-in in which 3 persons murthered (Trench Town Rock) and now I find myself in the position of those dead bodies: hands tied behind my back, feet x'd & bound, a wire round my neck! In the earlier case they used dishcloths, you may recall, from the Marley Manor clothesline since that was then an outside (al fresco) job. This time (inside) they used my telephone xtension chord; although it seems they used a **dishcloth** also: one that had fallen from my balcony (which they had entered my rooms from).

Last time—remember?—they used dishcloths to tie the 'moonlight' police up before they killed him. This time they used the cloth **to shit in**—at least that's the only xplanation for what we found next day upon the ground half-hid in flower-beds beneath the balcony: the whole thing wrapped up like a patty!

Dem gone with my **cyar** 2 colour **tvs** (the remote one the property of Marley Manor/but they had tief my own new new Remote that I had brought from Yale, from Barbican), the huge (ole fashion now) **IBM selectrix** that Mexican had type *Creole Society* on at Mecklenburgh Sq in London; **her wedding ring** from off my coward finger (the gunman whispered is dis GOLE?)—she gave me that in Georgetown 30 yrs ago. I never took it off; they almost broke it off; a **cassette/radio**, too many **tapes** (inc copy of my Bruce St John 'In Tribute' lecture & many of the H201 lectures that Chad had taped last year), a baby **calculator** from Air France (to Senegal), 4 **swatches**, 2 **torch lights** (one a very fancy one Kayiga wife helped me to buy at Harvard when I was coming back post-Gilbert), **binoculars** (I'd always wanted, like the one(s) at Round House), **money** too too much **money**, **telephone**, even 2 haffs of valium (they even went into my toilet bog) & at one time I thought they took my (only pair!) of **glasses**

ENTIRE little submarine is CHURNED up by the gunmen lookin money whe de money deh bwoy, gimme de money bwoy) *& whatever else to*

*cum & tek away.
They come in thru
a flimsy ungrilled
deregulated
balcon door (ply
wood & glass with
bolts no bigger
than small safety
pins at top of same
said door). Had
spoken to the
Marley Manor
Man/agement in*

vain about security. After the horse had bolted, as it were, they put on (two) large (larger) bolts: one at the top, one at the bottom of one side only of the two-leaf door. If they had SHOOT me as one of them had wisp me jess waaan

kill *smaddy twnite. It* **sweet** *me shoott you bwoy* **I wd have bleed to death upon that bed & been in there alone perhaps for days before Chad come to find me only in her dream…**

on this night of heavy intermittent rain & power cuts, had turned in early underneath the thunder. about 4:30—MM killing time—hear something wake me with a sense of like a door been open in the sitting room and like a

ANAMAL

was sniffing round. out there. glasses, torchlight, check this out. at bedroom door I see the sky/light—yes—door open—wha!—and then out of that dark room, a shove, obscenities, the metal thing with its round hole of death first hit me in the forehead, spin me round, pushing me *back into the bedroom with a tense voice whispering like* quiet bwoy (down rover down) *or we going* **shoot** *yu claat to rass: push shove gunbutt onto my only bed. face down my pillow pressed upon my only head: cuffs, gunbutts, tuffs at my locks etc &*whe de money, bwoy; *&* (more urgent) whe de money deh; *and later,* dese yu cyar keys? *& an xplanation (!) that dem needed it (the cyar) for going on a mission & that when dem finish, dem wd PHONE—* (gimme de numba hey—what

POWA

in dat gun—& TELL yu whe to pick it up again

that voice, as I write to you now & replay it & replay it once again, was MIDDLECLASS not ghetto stereotype. Despite the glot & argot style, it was the voice of someone who (why not?) had spent some clear-tongued years in a 'good' (secondary?) school (like) **"we have information that yu have money here…"**

but then I never see the voice of either face xcept just briefly once—too briefly to remember—& when I also see the knife (my kitchen knife? one of the stainless steel meat-cutting set I get as brahta from the Coop in Harvard Sq?) *which they now use to cut my t-phone wire so they cd tie me hand & foot & neck—like if they going to heng or strangle me—& stiff some claat inside me mouth —the Marley Man—or Xecution Style—*"now yu goin know how it will feel when we go

shoot

58

yu bwoy" and all this time my bright ears hearing like the rape of what was once my room: swishes & billows & clatterings down & then again & again somebody wd sit on the bed near my head with the hard & hot & cold of the gun at the back of my neck the other hand drowning me into the blackwater dark of the mattrass & whispering whispering **whe de money deh bwoy & yu goin sorry yu nevva tell we whe de money deh bwoy** *and when they had done—when they had gone—suitcases piled pillaged all over the place—my room like the sea—the debris & litter all over the beaches—bibliography files & my poetry manuscript folders all trampled & curled by the breakers—books hit by like a hurricane—what more can I tell you?—clothes torn from their hooks & their shoulders—my life like torn from its moorings & something like spiders crawling over my faces...*

and outside in the very normal dawnlight, not only the security guard no doubt sleepin safe (three months before don't forget he was cut up like meat in his 'station') *but OUR MAN VICTOR tell the police he had seen them running down the steps from my flat* (I mean with the tvs & ting?) *& even pushin my cyar out de yard since it doan start early a mornin these days & in fac one of them COME BACK UP when I thought they had gone, to ax me which key open up the door & VICTOR say that he see them hearsin my cyar away & thought, e say,* (I hear im tell the Police) *they was my own*

MECKANICS

is only when I got myself like free—had shuffled off the mortal coils of all the chords & wires & reached the bathroom window of my dreams to shout out FREEDOM to my neighbour—my wrists & ankles sullen swollen buked & abused & brazed for weeks to come— did Mr V come knock knock knocking on my door (the GUARD dem seh was SLEEPIN!) & one month after these events, one month & more of letters letters letters phonecalls all in a vain attempt to see the Chairman Person Owner Manor Manger Manager did me receive (19 Nov 90) a 'deep' & hand-delivered missile of 'concern' informing me that if I continue to feel threat at MMA, I 'should' (I quote) 'look into the possibility of alternate [sic] accomodation [sic]'

5. Short History of Dis

or

Middle Passages Today

Events that I here chronicle personwise or foolish cd have been recorded in various degrees—some less intense, some as you know far far more so—for other Caribbean countries & beyond. See Achebe, see Soyinka, see Biko, see Jackson, see Morislav Holub, see the *Diary of Anna Frank*, see Sun Yet Sun, see all the Disappeared of S America—*see see see until yu bline*

I remember Wilson Harris Mona 1968 on the eve of Black Power & Genet's **Blacks** departing from 'the green academy' of our campus with the 'smell *of carrion*' on his lips. I recall the night in 1975 when Brazil's conquering Santos came here to play before the hungry for them thousands at the Stadium. Pelé had scored a goal *olé* and all our world erupted. A young boy/man ran through the metal cordon of police—STATE OF EMERGENCY—and reached the maestro. Cheers

Going back. warm spille/ing all around his face. is knocked down by pursuit police onto the winning ground. A brown belt Superintendant of Police no less then kicks him in the face then kicks again to riff before the hundred thousand hungry live & tv eyes. It was Pelé who threw himself between the yout & that last brutal blow & hugged him to him. so

Another year. a gunshot. man bleeding. dead. face down in gutter right outside Tom Redcam's Public Libe. Shot by a Supercop or plainclothes JDF in pain broad daylight. And the police who came to 'pick him up'—he never bother stoop down to the brother. stood there & kicked my head until he bashed it in. until the kicking turned my body over. And no one in that lover crowd—like Pelé, MMA, *I cover the waterfront*—said anything said anything said anything Soon after that. news of another & another robbery with v.

another dead. another woman raped inside her house outside her house along the roadside going home from supermart from dancehall club from church from school. one poet friend of mine raped on the highway near the great greenheart traffic lights. another stoned to death on Stony Hill

The grills go up. the old nightwatchmen disappear. Welcome the red-tooth dog. the squat-face bodyguard. Those with good sense walk with their sawn-off shotguns. M16s & AK48s enter the rapidly declining currency of grace & courtesy. No Natty Dread but Natty Morgan hero of the nineteen-ninety-ninety-ones. Orlando Patto's Dungle of the 60s Sisyphus become the Riverton City (Kingston) Dump of 1992: an image of a city smouldering in garbage. & men & woman plundering that monstrous HELL of stench & detritus & death. dead rat. live rat. for bread. bone. dead rotting flesh. dead rotting fish. the decomposing contexts of yr kitchen sink & toilet bowl & latrine & what you sweep off from yr floor & doormat tabletop in greasy paper plastic bags

into that Dump goes the dead body of one University lecture & his woman frenn. profane cremation of the silence that surrounds that loss that no one hardly notices. The University itself says nothing since I suppose they'll say they DO NOT KNOW. They DO NOT KNOW who pays his salary or if his widow (is she?) gets his prison pension. His contract I suspect 'frustrated'/like Walter Rodney's was. And like the victims of our first (that 18th century) Middle Pass. no memory of no mourning for this passage

Bad Memories of Jubilee

or the half-hazard birthing of Caliban

> Tonia Byfield [herself an 'inmate' of the Jubilee Maternity Hospital]...said she witnessed some mothers undergoing painful experiences. One mother was ordered to go into the waiting room and sit there until the nurse attended to her. The baby's head appeared as the mother moaned. The nurses ignored her and she had to run to the delivery room with the baby head between her legs. Another mother, who had been in labour, said she went for a nurse on hearing the cry of [another] mother that [her] baby was on the way. She said the nurse merely said **'mek she stay down there an bawl.'** *SG* Nov 3, 1991

Human scavengers loot death car

By Claire Clarke
S Gleaner, 31 Mar 1991

With tracks of blood and brain marrow trailed around the site, a woman in the crowd excitedly captured a tube of lipstick from the wreckage. This young woman had also located a shoe saying, *"Mi like it, but mi nuh know whey de nex one dey."* Scanning the scene, she realized that the other foot was still inside the contorted machine of death; she attempted to close in and capture her prize, but the police intercepted, so for the time being she let it be.

This was not a scene from a movie showing the

depravity of the human condition, rather it was the scene of the GOOD FRIDAY NIGHT CAR ACCIDENT ALONG THE SP Tn ROAD IN Kgn which left two people dead.

The accident, which took place in the vicinity of the RIVERTON CITY DUMP, at approx 7:00 pm, attracted a crowd of curious and excited onlookers.

Human scavengers were quick to take what they cd from the twisted wreckage. By the time the SG team arrived... two tyres had already been removed from the vehicle.

Inside the car, no personal belongings were in sight save a lone ten cent... on the back seat. This too was removed.

22 [Professor] Aubrey Fraser [former Head of the Norman Manley Law School, UWI, Mona & prominent Caribbean legal luminary] was found dead in bed with his throat cut at his home in Jack's Hill, St Andrew, on the night of Nov 29 1988. The autopsy showed he had multiple [i.e 22] stab wounds to the neck, chest and behind the left ear and he had been bashed on the back of the head with the heavy procelain [sic] cover of a toilet tank
DG 12 Apr 91, p2
[By Dec 91, Fraser's wife & two of his chn were being charged w/his murder]

Shame of May Pen Cemetery
'Gone to the bones'

On Wednesday, on the second visit in a few days, a *Sunday Gleaner* team found the skeleton of a man who seemed to have been buried years ago. The skeletal remains were dressed in a pair of socks and blue pants. All that remained of him were the bones scattered on the ground nearby and the bones which remained inside his socks. The casket in which he was laid to rest was nowhere to be seen...

One mausoleum belonging to the late Bishop Mary Louise Coore stood as an old derelict structure. The concrete pillars supporting the roof had been crudely chopped into, the grilles dug out and the steel stolen leaving a mass of rubble and garbage on top of the grave...

On one visit by the team, smoke was seen spreading across the afternoon sky in the cemetery. On investigation, a large coal kiln was seen burning on top of a grave. Wood, presumably from the many trees in the cemetery, is cut, laid out on top and then sand is heaped over it, with the appropriate vent for lighting to produce firewood coal. Two other kilns, already "drawn", were built on other graves in this section. The coal burner, however, was nowhere to be seen...

This reporter [Misha Lobban] on Tuesday witnessed the theft of three goats that were tethered in an overgrown section of the cemetery. The lone robber escaped with them across the train line. The sorrowing owner, Joseph Williams, 81, who lives in Trench Town, stood helpless looking in the direction in which the thief had disappeared. He said the goats were valued at $1000.
Sun Gleaner 10 Nov 91

Chopping off Peoples Dreams

A WOMAN WHO STEPPED FROM A BUS IN THE PARADE AREA, DOWNTOWN KINGSTON, LOST AN ARM AND BRACELET TO ONE OF TWO MEN WHO CHOPPED OFF HER ARM, STOLE THE BRACELET OFF THE SEVERED ARM AND RAN AWAY.

EYEWITNESSES TOLD THE *TUESDAY STAR* THAT THE MID-AFTERNOON INCIDENT TWO WEEKS AGO WAS SWIFT AND DEADLY.

The *TUESDAY STAR* has learned that the woman who was wearing a thick bracelet stepped off the bus and into the path of a man armed with a meat chopper. Poised with the sharp weapon, the man inflicted a single blow which severed the woman's arm. When the arm fell to the ground, the man took it up, and while running, he removed the bracelet and threw away the arm. Eyewitnesses told the *TUESDAY STAR* that the woman fainted and was immediately removed from the scene by a passing motorist. **"When de hann drop, one a de man grab it up, and while running drag off de bracelet and dash wey de hann,"** an eyewitness said.

A nurse from the Bustamante Hospital for Children who said she witnessed the incident said, **"my blood run cold when I saw the woman fainted and the piece of arm began pulsating."**

THE MEN ESCAPED ALONG EAST QUEEN STREET.

THE *TUESDAY STAR* HAS BEEN TRYING TO IDENTIFY THE WOMAN WHO WAS SAID TO BE WEARING A TIGHTLY FITTED JEANS PANTS AND MULTI-COLOURED BLOUSE.

When *The Star* checked w/ various Kingston area hospitals about the woman, there was no information. A nurse at the Kingston Public went through the log for that day but found "no such case reported" there. The University Hospital said "we are not allowed to give out any information..." When contacted, a rep of the Nuttall Hospital asked, "What is her name? Are you a relative?" She added, "In any case it is not a policy to give out information like that."

>>Bloody Robbery/Robber flees with woman's arm<<

The Star/frontpage 17 Dec 1991

●

By now the Age of Dis. Distress Dispair & Disrespect. Distrust Disrupt Distruction. A Gardener cutlashes off a Helper's hand for saying that he shd not come in here & take Employer's food. The Friends he entertain laugh after him for letting Woman dis im

They break into our finest literary editor's home one night and place her carving knife between her teeth & force it forward. forward. forward. slicing the boundaries of skin that mark her lips that let her snark & smile & speak. until the dark blade reached the skull. You never knew a human tongue cd be so red & look so long & gurgle with such flame

Near where I write this now a man is training dogs to guard you or to kill you. seen? He stands in naked smoke in his ram/shack/le yard of galvanize & cast-off wood & kennels. a long whip in his leathered hand. his jackboots on. the animal like tied to him by leash & lash & violence. he grieves the dog an order & it dis/obeys. he hits it wham wham wham. the grey hound howls. the others writhe & crash against their cages in dis/pair. hout hout hout howl. the tails aggressive & yet crazy in their primal fear. he barks again. the animal howls back & dis/obeys. he strikes again again then strokes the fire. smoke. more smoke. a crackle in the fury. he strides within the noise he cannot hear & lashes out & howls & howls again

Does he have wife & children. mother. close friends. red distant relatives? what if he sees his dahta coming down the road? what if he hears his Grannie calling home?

The leashed dog howls like human baby in its terror. sparks squinting from its lurid tearless eye of error. wham wham wham wham. **command.** the salivating canine howls & leaps & tries to break away. the black whip turns it back & almost breaks its back. it howls again & staggers almost grovels as the Man commands. until the thin bitch whimpers. tail comes down. & falls. till in that silent yard. only the fire burns

6. Anansese

Anansese

Once when Ananse was a likkle bwoy he was goin on & im see PingWing Bramble wid a rat. Him fight Ping Wing tek way de rat so carry it heng up in de kitchen. When him was gawn Granny come een & eat off de rat. When Ananse come back, im cyaan fine de rat. Ananse seh, 'Come come Granny gi me me rat me rat come from PingWing PingWing come from God.' Granny seh, 'A cyaan gi yu back de rat because a heat it off, but tek dis knife'

Ananse go awn until im see a man was cuttin cane widout a knife. Im seh, 'Man, ow come yu cuttin cane widout a knife an I ave knife?' The man tek Ananse knife start cut de cane an bruk de knife

Ananse seh, 'Come come Man gi me me knife mi knife come from Granny Granny heat mi rat mi rat come from PingWing PingWing juk mi hann mi hann come from God'

De Man seh, 'A cyaan gi yu back yu knife for it breake. But tek dis grass'

Ananse go awn until im see Cow eatin dirt. Im seh, 'Ow yu eatin dirt an I ave grass?"

The cow tek de grass heat it off. Ananse seh, 'Come come Cow gi me mi grass mi grass come from Man Man bruk mi knife mi knife come from Granny Granny eat mi rat mi rat come from PingWing PingWing juk mi hann mi hann come from God'

Cow seh, 'Well a cyaan gi yu back yu grass but tek dis milk'

Ananse go on until im see a woman givin er baby black tea. Him seh, 'Ow yu givin yu baby black tea an I have milk'

The Woman tek de milk give it to er baby, baby drink it off

Ananse seh, 'Come come Woman gi me mi milk mi milk come from Cow Cow eat mi grass mi grass come from Man Man bruk mi knife mi knife come from Granny Granny eat mi rat mi rat come from PingWing PingWing juk mi hann mi hann come from God'

The woman seh, 'A cyaan gi yu back yu milk cause Baby drink it off, but tek dis blue..."

ᵥeom Neville Dawes, **The last enchantment** *(1960) & dedicated here to Yvonne Sobers who brought it first alive to us one afternoon in Ghana (1961)*